Table of Contents - Featured Articles

Staying Positive in a Negative World

Duane Cummings

The Importance of Attitude
10 Easy Steps to Make Yours Sensational!

Change your attitude and everything around you changes.

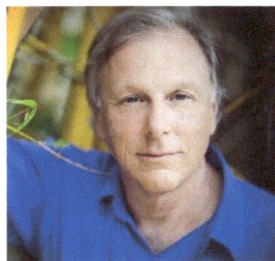

Alan Cohen

Truth or Sabotage?

Self-sabotage or sabotage of others occurs when you don't speak your truth directly. Honest expression of truth ends sabotage.

Debi Payne

How to Create a Positive Environment
Make a few simple changes to stay in a positive vibration.

Positive Tribe Magazine

Editor in Chief
Candi Parker

Contributors
Duane Cummings
Alan Cohen
Debi Payne
Judee Light
Karen Mayfield
James Clear
Teresa Velardi

Published by ParkerHouseBooks.com

This magazine is available at quantity discounts for bulk purchases and for branding by businesses and organizations - contact candi@parkerhousebooks.com

Table of Contents - continued

You can't live a

positive life

with a
negative mind.

Welcome From The Publisher

Welcome!

We are so happy and grateful that you are here!

It is our purpose and our pleasure to bring you the messages in these pages. Together we can raise the positive energy on this planet and make it a joy-filled place. If we each do this in our own environments, we can then grow towards each other and amplify the energy when we connect.

If you are feeling unfulfilled, dissatisfied, in pain or turmoil, then perhaps consciously choosing to be positive is something to consider. Close the door to negative thoughts.

It is our desire that you feel uplifted and more positive after you read these pages. So read on and let's see why our paths have crossed!

In Joy,

Candi Parker

Positive Thoughts Create Positive Realities

I dictate
the vibration
I am in.

Being positive is a state of mind.

It can be difficult to be, and stay, in a 'good' mood when events all around you are causing negative emotions to rise up and present themselves. We are constantly bombarded with salacious stories, horrific events, and fear mongering through the media and through word of mouth. Stored up negativity distorts our thinking and disconnects us from our bodies and from other people. It's hard to stay positive in these circumstances.

But staying positive in a negative world is easier than you think. First you have to decide that this is what you want to do. You must make a choice to practice being positive.

Old painful events from the past can cause irrational functioning in the present. When we reclaim our ability to feel positive and develop the ability to release any buildup of negativity, we will then be in a position to function in the world with a clearer mind and a happier heart. Your mind is actually shaping the world around you. What you think about you bring about.

When you feel negative you tend to focus on what is wrong, always looking for the flaw. There is also a tendency to recount, over and over, negative events and situations with anyone who will commiserate with you. You may look for people to listen to you as you download all of the negative emotions you can't quite keep inside anymore.

When you feel positive more often than not you see the good in situations. You tend to look for, and talk about, funny, happy and positive things. You feel more at peace with the world around you.

When you feel negative you tend to hold yourself expressing this, your shoulders may be hunched causing tightness, a frown or a scowl on your face, your arms may be crossed and you may be hunched over a little and always looking for what is wrong.

When you feel positive the feeling is more expansive, in how you hold yourself. When you are more positive you hold your head up higher, you stand up straighter, you may have a relaxed face or a smile, you are more open. Being that way allows your body to function better, more properly. The flows in your body, mind and spirit are better, which means better health, and a better feeling about your health.

If you find that you are having difficulty getting into or maintaining a positive attitude, here are some things you can do right now to help shift you...

- Go on a news fast. Stop listening to the news. If you haven't noticed, the daily news is very skewed towards negativity and sensationalism. If something disastrous is headed your way, trust me, someone will tell you about it.

- Find positive material to put around you. Use positive messages that resonate with you. Put them on post-its or cardboard and place them everywhere you will notice them like the refrigerator, on the mirrors, next to the toilet, next to your bed, etc.

▪ Be an uplifter. Look for ways to uplift others. Because when you uplift other people it bounces right back to you and it lifts you.

▪ Clear your vibration and your environment. You can meditate, do yoga, get a massage...whatever will give you a peaceful mood. And clear clutter for clarity. Clean your environments and put a plant or two around as they give off oxygen.

▪ Do something that makes you laugh. Watch comedy or funny movies. Find a laughter yoga group in your area. Go to laughteryoga.org. to find a place near you and learn more about laughter yoga.   Call up your funny friends. How many times a day do you smile? Physically, smiling releases endorphins and dopamine into your system, which creates a feeling of well-being. It is good for your body, mind, and spirit.

See part two in the next issue...

Candi Parker is a certified Law of Attraction coach, author, book publisher, book coach, Acupuncture Physician and Army veteran. As well as being a serial entrepreneur, she leads the Tallahassee chapter of the Women's Prosperity Network.

Her book, *Shift Happens: How I Won a Million Dollars with the Law of Attraction* is on Amazon in print and on Kindle.

The common theme in all she does is her passion and expertise in providing ways for people to achieve health, wealth and happiness. *www.CandiParker.com*

Here's the key...

Your circumstances
change according
to your thoughts.

~ Candi Parker

The Importance of Attitude:
10 Easy Steps to Make Yours Sensational!

It has been said that "Attitude is everything." Although I haven't confirmed it yet, I can assure you it is at the top of my list. Any successes or miss-steps I have had in my life were driven by my attitude. Over time, I learned our attitudes are a direct reflection of our actions. So, if you want to change your attitude, you should start by changing your actions. We need to understand that it is our physiology that most influences our attitude. The way we stand, move and even breath determines our mental state and subsequently our attitude.

Duane Cummings

Unlike personality, attitudes are expected to change as a function of experience. Most attitudes are the result of either direct experience or observed learning from our environment. Your attitude isn't "what" happens to you; it is how you represent it to yourself and respond. Because you decide how to respond to those events, your attitude becomes a choice. So, if you have the ability to choose your attitude, why not select to have a sensational one. I am sure there are many other ways to achieve a sensational attitude, but here are my ten favorites. I continue to use these steps so that I may live a Sensational Life.

1.) Surround yourself with Positive People. My mother use to say, "You are who you hang out with." Those people around you will have a big impact on what you value and how you think. Eliminate the "Negative Nellie's!"

The Sensational Salesman
A Second Chance Story: Providing a Simple Path to Improving Your Relationships, Career, and Life

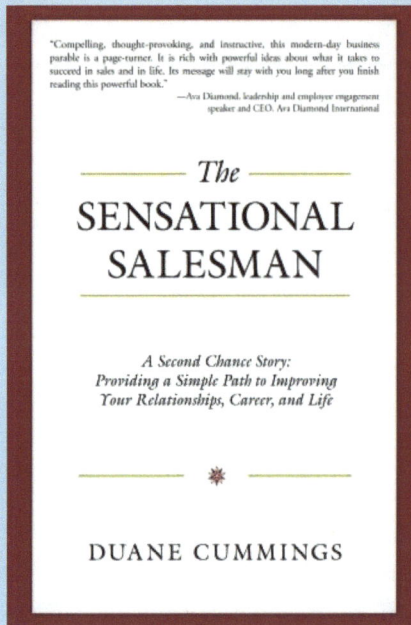

Lots of books claim they will change your life, but they rarely give you a map to follow. If you have been searching for answers about how to improve your current situation, look no further. Duane Cumming's book, *The Sensational Salesman,* serves as a must-have manual for achieving success in business and life. The insights in this story are rarely taught in formal education settings or the workplace, but they are fundamental to achieving lifelong happiness and fulfillment.

This is the inspiring parable of Thomas Frickle, a young salesman whose life quickly unravels, only to be put back on course thanks to the help of mentors who teach him crucial lessons. It is entertaining and easy to follow. With lessons on topics such as relationships, communication, and goal setting, this story will provide you with a step-by-step blueprint for how to achieve the personal and professional success you desire and deserve. Even the most educated mind will be enlightened by the way the key building blocks needed for success in all aspects of your life are presented here. Each chapter reveals a new lesson, building on the previous one and utilizing real world examples that you can begin applying immediately. This is a timeless story and a valuable book for young and old alike.

Amazon.com, Barnes and Noble and fine bookstores everywhere

2.) _Learn something new every day._ You can encourage a Sensational Attitude by expanding yourself. My Grandfather used to say, "Do something, even if it is wrong." What he meant was experience life. Take a night class, study a new language, and learn to garden or anything else that interests you. Most people don't regret what they have done; they regret what they never did.

3.) _Slow down and get back to the basics._ Call an old friend, play with a pet, visit an interesting place or listen to your favorite music. You can also take a walk, read a book, take a long bath, or sit and play with children. Sometimes it is the simplest things in life that give us pleasure and remind us what is most important.

4.) _Find someone to help._ Whether you volunteer with an organization or just provide a random act of kindness, the act of helping others can give you joy and purpose. You may also find that you realize how lucky you are compared to some and become more thankful. You will also find a higher level of self-worth when you begin investing in other people.

5.) _Accept the fact that things will not always go your way._ If you always expect things to go perfectly, you probably spend a great deal of time being disappointed. Keeping a level head and understanding that things will go wrong and finding more productive ways to handle the situation will instantly improve your attitude. There is nothing wrong with aiming for the stars, but if you don't reach them, at least enjoy the sky around you, reduces the chances of stroke, high blood pressure and heart attacks.

6.) _Include laughter in your daily diet._ Whether you learn to laugh at yourself and the mistakes you make, take in a funny movie, or you go out to enjoy professional comedians, laughter is truly the best medicine. I also recommend that you learn to tell jokes. You will get a great deal of pleasure from making other people smile and laugh. It is a scientific fact that laughter reduces the chances of stroke, high blood pressure and heart attacks.

7.) _Limit your exposure to mainstream media._ Much of the regular nightly news is negative. They focus on information that can create an attachment to fear, negative thoughts and negative emotion. You can get important news from sources that present it in a more positive platform. Be active and filter what goes into your brain and nervous system.

8.) _Program your own mind and emotions._ Rather than allowing yourself to glide through life on autopilot, take control. You decide what goes into your mind by selecting books or CDs that provide positive messages and stories. Visit websites and places that are sharing inspirational stories of success and triumph rather than those of doom and failure. Schedule time to listen to speakers at events that will help you achieve rather than demoralize and handicap you.

9.) _Get some exercise._ You need to find physical activities you enjoy and can perform regularly. Not only is it a social avenue to experience other people, but also it has obvious benefits to your physical well-being and your mental health. Regular exercise is a major tool in combating depression and will regulate your body chemistry to aid in improving your overall mood.

10.) _Use Positive language._ YOU are the words you use. How you speak to others and how they speak to you is important. Maybe even more important is how you speak to yourself. You need change your self-talk to ensure you are supportive and do not limit yourself. Stop saying, "Why does this always happen to me?" and start asking questions like, "How can I learn from this and ensure it doesn't happen any longer?"

Duane Cummings is the founder of The Sensational Group. He is a successful business owner and has been involved in sales and management coaching, mentoring and training for over 25 years. Duane is also author of the new professional development book, **_The Sensational Salesman._**

He can be reached at duane@thesensationalgrp.com You can learn more about Duane and The Sensational Company at thesensationalgrp.com

Truth or Sabotage?

Alan Cohen

Alan brings a warm blend of wisdom, intimacy, humor, and vision to the path of personal, professional, and spiritual growth. He loves to extract lessons from the practical experiences of daily living, and find beauty in the seeming mundane. Many readers and seminar participants have reported that his teachings have brought them deep encouragement and empowerment, and inspired them to believe in themselves and achieve new levels of success in their personal and professional life.

I work with a rental car agency that gets me good deals. When I began to use the agency I phoned in an order to the owner, who is a friend of mine. When he emailed me the confirmation, I discovered he made an error on the pickup time of the car. I called him back and he corrected it. This happened not just once, but three times. Hmmm.

I told the agent that I planned to recommend his service for participants of my residential retreats. He told me, "Great! Just be sure to have them book online—that's a lot easier for me than processing a phoned reservation."

Suddenly I realized why the agent had consistently messed up my orders. He didn't want to take phone orders. His errors were subterfuge ways of saying, "I don't want to do this." When he finally told me the truth, I was happy to change the way I ordered. But he had to tell me the truth first.

We all seek to express our truth. We all *must* express our truth. There are two ways to express your truth: directly or indirectly. If you do not express your truth directly, it will come out in odd, aberrant, and damaging ways. Self-sabotage or sabotage of others occurs when you don't speak your truth directly. Honest expression of truth ends sabotage.

I had an office assistant whom I asked to pick up a laser printer cartridge on her way home from work one day, and she agreed. The next day when she came to work I asked her for the cartridge. "I couldn't find the shop," she told me. We found a map to the shop and she went off that day after work to find it. The following day she again returned empty-handed. "I got there after they closed," she reported. I let her off work early that day to make it to the shop on time. The next day she told me, "I forgot to bring the company credit card."

Finally I picked up the cartridge myself without a hitch. The truth my assistant resisted telling me was, "I don't want to do this." I wish she would have told me that up front; it would have saved both of us time and trouble. When you don't tell the truth up front, your truth comes out in weird ways that make more trouble for everyone.

We all have the ability to do anything we choose to do—IF we choose to do it. The story is told about Joe, who came home from work one day quite tired. As he was unwinding in front of his TV during the evening, Joe's buddy phoned him and asked Joe if he would help him move his refrigerator. "I'd sure like to," Joe answered, "but I had a tough day at work and I'm beat. Maybe another time."

Ten minutes later Joe received a phone call from his girlfriend, who had just gotten back into town after being away on a business trip. "I'm back, honey," she told Joe. "I just got a new Victoria's Secret lingerie outfit. Would you like to come over and help me try it out?"

Did Joe suddenly have energy? *You bet!* He wasn't lying to his buddy when he said he was too tired. He was too tired because he wasn't motivated. We all find the energy and means to do what we choose to do. We find no energy to do the things we do not want to do. If we are forced to do things we do not want to do, we will find a way not to do them. That's how powerful we are. The question is, will you express your preference honestly, or will you create veiled situations to get your point across?

You don't have to get sick to get out of school, have an accident to get out of work, or have an affair to get out of a marriage. You can simply, clearly, directly express that you do not wish to do this. You might ruffle some feathers, but the cost will be far less than illness, accident, or a nasty divorce. Yet there is a hidden value in direct communication. You might create a solution that surpasses simply staying unhappily or leaving dramatically. By expressing your feelings you might be able to change schools, transfer departments at work, or deepen your intimacy, connection, and reward in marriage. Truth has ways of getting to solutions that sabotage does not.

Ceanne Derohan wrote a classic book entitled, *Right Use of Will.* We are always using our will. But we may not always be using it in alignment with our good. Your will is like an automobile with its engine running and the gearshift in drive. You can steer the car onto the main highway and take the most direct route to where you want to go. Or you can drive it through many detours and byways, over bumps and through walls. Ultimately you will get to your destination, but one path is a lot more direct and fun than another.

The universe rewards authenticity. Things are *supposed* to go right, and they usually do. When you say yes to what you choose, and no to what you do not choose, you are living in alignment with yourself.

Life asks no more—or less—of you than this.

Alan Cohen is the author of many popular inspirational books, including *Enough Already: The Power of Radical Contentment*. Join Alan for his acclaimed Life Coach Training to become a professional life coach or incorporate life coaching skills in your current career. For more information about this program, Alan's other books, free daily inspirational quotes, and his weekly radio show, visit www.alancohen.com, email info@alancohen.com, or phone (800) 568-3079 or (808) 572-0001.

IT'S ALL GOOD

Looking on the Bright Side!

> "When something happens in your life that looks or feels "bad", what is your first inclination? To resist it? To say: "Oh, no! Poor me?" or "Why me?" Or, do you say: "This is not what I expected, yet I know there is a gift in it, so I'm keeping my eyes open for it!""

Judee Light

is a speaker, teacher, author, editor, F.U.N. facilitator, and adventure lover with over 33 years' experience. She is a fourth generation Unity student and has been speaking at Unity churches for over 22 years. She is the author of the book, When I Let Go and Let God. You can find out more about her and what she is about at FeelingUpliftedNow.com (F.U.N.)

Does it seem like lots of "bad" appearing things have been happening on the planet and in the lives of people you know, and maybe in your life in the last lately?

Our planet is transforming, we are transforming, and a lot of things are coming up to be dealt with . . . to be, let go of or to be looked at in a new way. We often think we see the truth, yet we only see the truth as we perceive it to be, based on our past conditioning and on our belief systems.

I am grateful that my parents taught me at a young age that "everything happens for best." I believed them (for they were my parents!) and so I looked for the best in every situation, especially in those that didn't feel good at first, and I still do. When I do this, the Law of Attraction goes into action and starts bringing me the best, and often in ways that I could never have imagined!

**Remember that every moment is a new moment.
If you have things in your life that are not looking or feeling so good to you now, you have the choice and power to look at them differently, to see anew.**

We're always at possibility junction. We can always choose again (from the field of all possibilities). We can always choose our attitude, the way we look at something, if our first automatic knee-jerk reaction does not feel good.

Some experiences seen from the human level seem to *obstruct*. And seen from a higher level, we know they are here to *instruct*. What if you realized that so-called obstacles are not opposing you, but merely re-routing you?

Dr. Bernie Siegel said that when he was young and something unexpected happened that he didn't want, his mother would say, "Bernie, God is redirecting you."

It is important not to judge that which seems to stand in your way as your "enemy". It can often be your best friend, sending you on a detour that takes you around what could have been your biggest stumbling block.

Feel gratitude for and bless anything or anyone that appears to be opposing you, as all things happen for good. When you do this, you let go of preconceived notions (the past) and open up your mind to new possibilities.

Practice looking on the bright side . . . looking for the silver linings, looking on the feel-good side. The shifts described below are some changes in perception I have learned to make over the years that change my feelings from heavy to lighter and brighter and thus create more happiness and success in my life. If they work for me, they can work for you, too:

Heavy Feeling	Lighter Brighter Feeling
Problem (something to overcome)	Challenge (something to meet) Opportunity for growth "Here I grow again!"
Mistake	Learning experience
Failure	(is simply quitting too soon) "I didn't get the result I wanted. So I go to Plan B! or X , Y or Z!" It's just part of the process of success. So-called failures are stepping stones to success.
I quit, got fired, got divorced	"I graduated (from this job, marriage)! I learned a lot and I'm moving up to the next higher level!"
I'll try (struggle, effort, doubt)	I intend that . . . (leverage the Law of Attraction and inspired action)
Stepmother/stepfather/stepchild	Bonus mother/bonus father/bonus child
Belated birthday greeting	Extended birthday greeting
This is to die for.	"This is to live for!"
That's unbelievable! (when something good happens)	"I believe it!" (accept it and allow it)
Disaster victims	Hurricane/earthquake/flood survivors
Betrayal	A call to higher consciousness
Fear	A reminder that I'm focusing on what I don't want (instead of what I do want)

Pain, anger, fear, sadness	Energy (e-motion = energy in motion, let it move)
Chaos, confusion	Signs of growth and transformation!
I feel like I "hit a wall". I'm in darkness.	"Here I grow again." "Breakthrough is almost here! I'm 75% of the way to my goal!"
I'm losing it.	"The dawn is coming!" (darkness is a period of incubation, a hidden growth period)
I'm going backwards My life is falling apart!	"I've mastered one level, and am now on the next level and I am a beginner here." "I'm backing up for a running leap!"
You need to be realistic!	"My life is really coming together at a higher level!" "You're talking about historical reality. I'm creating a new reality."
You're crazy!	Two meanings for "crazy": extraordinary, unbound (free) "Yes, I'm crazy all right!"

Alan Cohen says, "Seen properly, the tale of woe becomes a tale of wow!" So start telling new stories about you and your life.

Stretton Smith says, "We're not here to *set* it right. We're here to *see* it right!

Be one who lives on the bright side and tells tales of "Wow"! Be one who sees your life right and who lives a life of Wow!

FeelingUpliftedNow.com
(F.U.N.).

How To Create A Positive Environment

" In order to maintain a positive attitude, it is important to create a positive environment that will surround you 24/7.

Debi Payne

Debi Payne is the artist and designer behind Debi Payne Designs focusing on artwork and product design emphasizing positive words and affirmations. You can view the Debi Payne Designs line of products in her Inspiration Station online store.

DebiPayneDesigns.com

To set up a positive environment you will need to first look at the environment currently surrounding you. Spend a full day paying close attention to everything typically around you. Pay close attention to the images and words in your environment that you see and are impressing on your mind day after day.

Once you start paying close attention and becoming aware of the things that surround you everyday, you may find that you need to make more than just a few changes. When you wake up in the morning, what is the first thing that you see? How long are you awake before you see, read or hear something positive? For most people, as soon as they wake up the first thing they do is look at a clock to see what time it is. Have on the nightstand by that clock a small picture frame where you have written on a piece of paper the words, "It's a GREAT day!" That way, before you are even out of bed the first message your brain has received is that it is a great day. With that piece of information, you brain mind will begin to set out doing everything that it can to make the day great.

Think about all the things and products you use throughout the day. Are they helping you to create a positive environment? Do you drink coffee from the same cup every morning?

Try using a cup that has a positive word or affirmation. Every time you pick up your keys to go somewhere, attach a key ring with a positive word or affirmation to serve as a reminder to stay positive. If you have an office job and work at a computer all day, why not have a mouse pad with a positive word or affirmation that you can look at all day long.

Creating a positive environment can actually be a lot of fun. Once you start looking at the things already around you and deciding how you can change them, the more things you will look for to change. You can also make little games to play throughout the day. Write the word "gratitude" on a piece of paper or a post it note and put it on the bathroom mirror or on the refrigerator. Every time you see the word "gratitude" immediately stop what you are doing and say out loud three things that you are grateful for.

Another idea is to take a bottle of water and remove the label. Next you can either make a new band label to go around the bottle or you can use a sharpie pen and write directly on the bottle. Write a positive word in large letters, like "success", "prosperity", "good health", or whatever you want more of in your life. Then as you are drinking the water think to yourself, "I am drinking in success" or "I am drinking in good health."

> By making just a few simple changes throughout your normal day, you will quickly find how much easier it is to stay in a positive vibration and you will see how quickly things start shifting in a positive way for you.

See her products at zazzle.com/inspiration_station

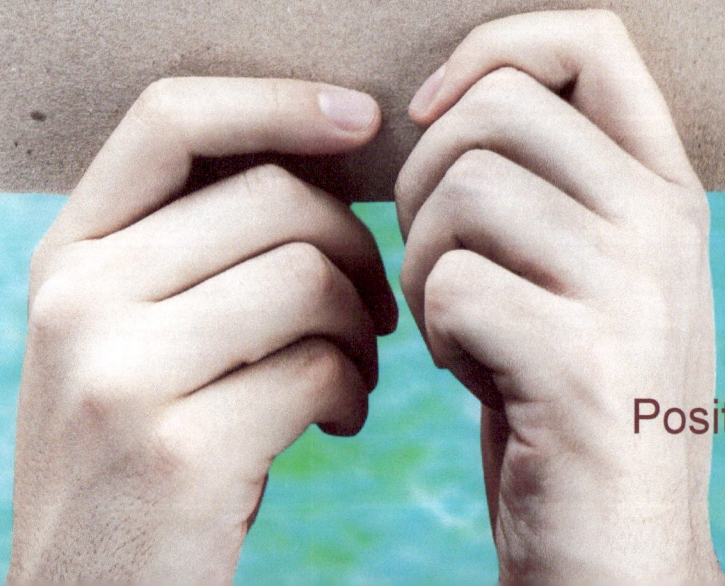

POSITIVE THINGS HAPPEN TO POSITIVE PEOPLE

PositiveTribe.com

Random Acts of Giving for Change

Karen Mayfield

Karen Mayfield is a bestselling author, speaker, metaphysical minister, Spiritual Life Coach. and founder of Wake up Women. Karen takes you into the world and brand of Wake up Women while guiding you through your process of waking up to your life of happiness, health & wealth, with Peace of mind to live the life you love. To learn more about Karen visit
www.wakeupwomen.com

Several years ago, while driving back home from a weekend with my family 160 miles away from my home, my gas light came on indicating that I had about 47 miles to empty. And here I was still about 80 miles from home. I pulled off the highway at the next exit to get gas and realized I had no money of any kind with me. After searching my car I was able to gather up about $1.60 in loose change. I had found just enough money to get just enough gas to get home without running out.

While sitting in the parking lot of the gas station, I see this battered looking woman in cut-offs running toward my car. As she gets closer, I can tell she is bleeding and has several physical injuries. She nears my car and I can tell she is panicking and needs some help. As she tells me her story of being pushed out of the car by her boyfriend while going 50 MPH and rolling head over heels for about 20 feet before landing in the ditch, I was ready to help her any way I could. Her only need was enough change to call from the payphone to get someone to come and pick her up and take her to the hospital. Without even thinking I gave her my last $1.60 for her to make her call and I waited with her until her sister came to get her.

When we give for giving
we will always have
more than we need.

~ Karen Mayfield

Now, once again, I'm faced with no money and no gas so, with just a leap of faith, I get back on the freeway and head home. After all, I still had 47 miles to empty so I would be 47 miles closer to home when I run out of gas. Interestingly, that gas stretched to cover the 80 miles! By the grace of GOD, I made it to within 3 blocks of my house. I had to coast off of the freeway at my exit. I coasted into a gas station over on the side and out of the way. I was just going to walk home and told the attendant in the gas station that I would be back in the morning to pick up my car. After gathering up all my stuff, as I was getting out of my car I dropped my keys and they fell into the side pocket of the car door. I reached in to get the keys and I found something else - a five dollar bill! I was perplexed to say the least because I had skimmed every inch of the car earlier for money to buy gas and there was no five dollars in the car door! So where did it come from? I just looked out the windshield and gave a big thank you to God.

I will always remember that experience because it was then and there I knew the power of giving for giving. My Grandmother always told me the story of giving the shirt off of your back and having someone give you a complete wardrobe of clothes.

When we give to get we will be left wanting, but when we give for giving we will always have more than we need.

If you have a giving story please share it with us at support@positivetribe.com with 'giving story' in the subject line.

The first place we lose the battle is in our own thinking. If you think it's permanent then it's permanent. If you think you've reached your limits then you have. If you think you'll never get well then you won't. You have to change your thinking. You need to see everything that's holding you back, every obstacle, every limitation as only temporary.

~ Joel Olsteen

How Positive Thinking Builds Your Skills, Boosts Your Health, and Improves Your Work

James Clear

My work is focused on a simple idea: I want to share practical ideas and proven research that helps you master your habits, optimize your performance, and take control of your health and happiness.

I share my writing, my photography, and my books at JamesClear.com.

P ositive thinking sounds useful on the surface. (Most of us would prefer to be positive rather than negative.) But, "positive thinking" is also a soft and fluffy term that is easy to dismiss. In the real world, it rarely carries the same weight as words like "work ethic" or "persistence."

But those views may be changing. Research is beginning to reveal that positive thinking is about much more than just being happy or displaying an upbeat attitude. Positive thoughts can actually create real value in your life and help you build skills that last much longer than a smile.

The impact of positive thinking on your work, your health, and your life is being studied by people who are much smarter than me. One of these people is Barbara Fredrickson. Fredrickson is a positive psychology researcher at the University of North Carolina and she published a landmark paper that provides surprising insights about positive thinking and it's impact on your skills. Her work is among the most referenced and cited in her field and it is surprisingly useful in everyday life.!

Let's talk about Fredrickson's discovery and what it means for you...

What Negative Thoughts Do to Your Brain!

Play along with me for a moment.

Let's say that you're walking through the forest and suddenly a tiger steps onto the path ahead of you. When this happens, your brain registers a negative emotion — in this case, fear.

Researchers have long known that negative emotions program your brain to do a specific action. When that tiger crosses your path, for example, you run. The rest of the world doesn't matter. You are focused entirely on the tiger, the fear it creates, and how you can get away from it.

For example, when you're in a fight with someone, your anger and emotion might consume you to the point where you can't think about anything else. Or, when you are stressed out about everything you have to get done today, you may find it hard to actually start anything because you're paralyzed by how long your to–do list has become. Or, if you feel bad about not exercising or not eating healthy, all you think about is how little willpower you have, how you're lazy, and how you don't have any motivation.

In each case, your brain closes off from the outside world and focuses on the negative emotions of fear, anger, and stress — just like it did with the tiger. Negative emotions prevent your brain from seeing the other options and choices that surround you. It's your survival instinct.

Now, let's compare this to what positive emotions do to your brain. This is where Barbara Fredrickson returns to the story.

What Positive Thoughts Do to Your Brain

Fredrickson tested the impact of positive emotions on the brain by setting up a little experiment. During this experiment, she divided her research subjects into 5 groups and showed each group different film clips.

The first two groups were shown clips that created positive emotions. Group 1 saw images that created feelings of joy. Group 2 saw images that created feelings of contentment.

The last two groups were shown clips that created negative emotions. Group 4 saw images that created feelings of fear. Group 5 saw images that created feelings of anger. Afterward, each participant was asked to imagine themselves in a situation where similar feelings would arise and to write down what they would do. Each participant was handed a piece of paper with 20 blank lines that started with the phrase, "I would like to…"

Participants who saw images of fear and anger wrote down the fewest responses. Meanwhile, the participants who saw images of joy and contentment, wrote down a significantly higher number of actions that they would take, even when compared to the neutral group. In other words, negative emotions narrow your mind and focus your thoughts. At that same moment, you might have the option to climb a tree, pick up a leaf, or grab a stick — but your brain ignores all of those options because they seem irrelevant when a tiger is standing in front of you!

This is a useful instinct if you're trying to save life and limb, but in our modern society we don't have to worry about stumbling across tigers in the wilderness. The problem is that your brain is still programmed to respond to negative emotions in the same way — by shutting off the outside world and limiting the options you see around you!

Let's consider a real–world example.

 A child who runs around outside, swinging on branches and playing with friends, develops the ability to move athletically (physical skills), the ability to play with others and communicate with a team (social skills), and the ability to explore and examine the world around them (creative skills). In this way, the positive emotions of play and joy prompt the child to build skills that are useful and valuable in everyday life.

These skills last much longer than the emotions that initiated them. Years later, that foundation of athletic movement might develop into a scholarship as a college athlete or the communication skills may blossom into a job offer as a business manager. T he happiness that promoted the exploration and creation of new skills has long since ended, but the skills themselves live on.

Fredrickson refers to this as the "broaden and build" theory because positive emotions *broaden* your sense of possibilities and open your mind, which in turn allows you to *build* new skills and resources that can provide value in other areas of your life.

In the next issue, James Clear teaches
How to Increase Positive Thinking in Your Life

Conversations That Make a Difference: Shift Your Beliefs To Get What You Want

Whether you live in a basement with the income of a lemonade stand entrepreneur or in the South of Wales on a vineyard surrounded by the finest grapes and beautiful views, your belief will limit you or set you free. Belief is the strongest force in the universe yet it exists only in the mind. Look at your life —

- Are you physically fit and on top of your game?

- Financially do you struggle to make ends meet?

- Emotionally are you prone to breakdowns, depression and feel like a failure?

- Spiritually are you numbed by the world, empty and void of the connections that feed your soul?

- Are you doing what you love, fueling your passions and fulfilling your purpose?

- Are you happy in your relationships with others?

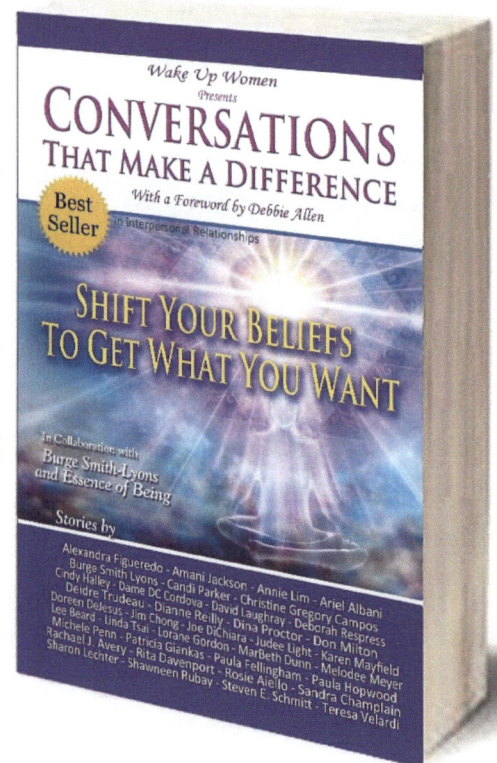

This compelling page turner is filled with wisdom that may trigger a shift in you and create the momentum needed to shift your beliefs and get what you want. It all begins and ends with the conversation you have with yourself that will make the difference.

www.ConversationsThatMakeaDifference.com

Five Keys to Living in Gratitude

> What is gratitude? Webster's dictionary defines it at *a feeling of appreciation or thanks.* I say it's an attitude.

Teresa Velardi

is an Author, Editor, Speaker, Potter and Transformational Life Coach.
Bring out the greatness within you as you discover that you already have the ability to shift every aspect of your life into high gear! Uncover the Dynamic person within and wake up to your most powerful, prosperous and passionate life.
Learn more about Teresa at
www.teresavelardi.com
and
www.wakeupwomen.com
or email her at
teresavelardi@gmail.com

I believe that gratitude is the key that unlocks the door to abundance in every area of our lives. How do we keep that feeling of gratitude alive throughout our lives? Let me offer you five keys to living a life of gratitude. I invite you to use them in developing your own attitude of gratitude.

1. Practice Humility

Humility is the quality or state of not thinking you are better than other people; the quality of being humble. I believe it is the opposite of arrogance. Arrogant people, in my experience have an attitude that the world owes them something just because they are alive. Arrogance is defined as *an insulting way of thinking or behaving that come from believing that you are better, smarter, or more important than other people.* They are also pretentious and proud

Humble people are modest and courteously respectful. They are people who know the meaning of being of service and in service to others. A humble person will give generously and graciously receive, where as an arrogant one will reflect the air of entitlement.

A Grateful Heart is a Humble Heart

2. Count Your Blessings Daily

It's really easy to get caught up in this world of "I want more," or "I need more." What about that which you already have? Do you really need another (whatever)?

Don't you have one just like it in the closet? Think about those who have so little. In this time when there are still so many people jobless and homeless, do you feel grateful for what you have? When was the last time you counted your blessings?

Putting the material things to the side, what about the people in your life? Do you let them know that you appreciate them? That you are grateful for their friendship? Or that you are happy that someone is your parent, your sibling, your cousin, or maybe your classmate or associate at work?

Far too often, we take others and the things that we have for granted. In so many nations around the world, people have nothing in comparison to what we have. Recently, I was given the opportunity to talk to some young children from Kenya. I was in awe of the joy in these children. They have nothing, and many days, they have no food. Until recently, they had no fresh water supply. Imagine your life without water or food.

To count your blessings means to recognize all the good that you have in your life. When we consciously do this every day, we are developing our attitude of gratitude. We must first realize and be grateful for the already abundant life we have, no matter how much or how little that is before more will be given. And for some reason the more you live in gratitude, the more you have.

Counting your blessings helps to develop an attitude of gratitude and recognition of abundance.

3. Keep a Gratitude Journal

This is something I have been doing for years now. Every day I write down at least 3 things that I am grateful for. I begin with I am so happy and grateful for (whatever). I'm not the first one to do this. As a matter of fact, I think Bob Proctor is the one who teaches people to write that they are "Happy and Grateful". Believe it or not, just writing those words causes me to feel happy and grateful even if I wasn't when I opened my journal.

I challenge myself to think of things outside of the stuff I was writing every day like the warm bed I had slept in, the roof over my head, the air that I breathe. I found myself not 'stretching' my mind to look for things outside of

my immediate surroundings. One way to step out of the box of everyday things to put on your list is to play the A to Z Gratitude game. Use each letter of the alphabet, one every day to create your list of things and people you are grateful for. When you see the things you're grateful for on the page each day, it gives new perspective.

Keep a Gratitude Journal. You can also post your daily gratitude list here: http://bit.ly/gratefulhearts

4. Spend Time in Prayer and Meditation

No matter who or what you call a higher power in your life, spending time in connection with source is an important part of living gratefully. For me, God is the provider of all and makes all things possible. I remember a song from when I was a child with these words "Seek ye first the kingdom of God, and his righteousness, and all these things shall be added unto you", from the bible verse, Matthew 6:33. The more I look to God, the more he blesses my life.

That's my own experience, and many people who I have talked to throughout my life claim the same truth. Someone once told me that prayer is my part of the conversation and that meditation is the quiet within which I can hear God's part. Believing that all things come from God, and spending time with God gives a sense of great gratitude, and a sense of connection.

So no matter what your belief is, spending time in prayer and meditation offers the opportunity to feel grateful for that source, a sense of connection, and a feeling of quiet within, a feeling of peace. Pray for peace too.

5. Share it With Someone Else

While you are counting your blessings, writing in your gratitude journal and playing the gratitude game or while in your quiet meditation time you may come upon the name of someone you haven't talked to in a while, give them a call and let them know that you are grateful for them today. I recently had this happen to me, and the person was so glad to hear my voice. We had a great conversation, and caught up on what had been happening in our lives. We were BOTH grateful for the conversation and the renewed connection

Pay if forward. When you are going through things that you no longer need, instead of throwing them out, why not give them to an organization that will use them to help another. Gently used coats and clothing are collected by a number of organizations. Do you have old glasses? Seek out people who will recycle them to the elderly or the homeless. What about that cell phone you just replaced? Women's shelters set these phones up as emergency phones that dial 911. You never know if that old phone will save someone's life. What about blankets, and housewares? Far too many people live their lives on the streets or in shelters. Any and all of these things that you may have thrown out can help someone else.

Being grateful for what you have, and then paying forward to someone else who will use it really warms the heart, gratitude is contagious, so share your attitude of gratitude with someone else!

I'm grateful for you!

Color Me Positive Coloring Book is a collection of coloring pages around positive messages. As you are coloring, your subconscious is taking in the positive message and in turn you may experience a more positive attitude. Coloring gently helps you to de-stress from the day and allows you to release negative thoughts by focusing your mind on the present moment.

Featuring:
• A variety of coloring designs with positive messages meant to evoke peace and positivity.

• Images are on one side only to protect the designs under it and to be able to remove your beautifully colored positive message and frame it.

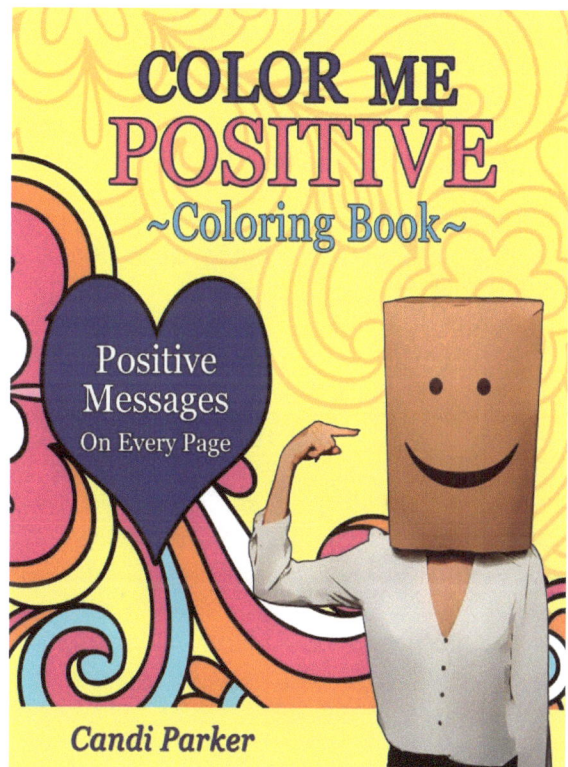

• Simple to complex designs for your every mood.

Great Gift!

Available now
On Amazon.com

For Hippies of All Ages!

Coloring gently helps you to de-stress from the day and allows you to release negative thoughts by focusing your mind on the present moment. The growing trend of grown-up coloring books is fast becoming one of the most popular ways to relax.

Featuring:
- 36 Groovy designs
- A variety of coloring designs meant to evoke peace, happiness, grins and giggles.
- Images are on one side only to protect the designs under it and to be able to remove your beautifully colored artwork and frame it.
- Simple to complex designs for your every mood.

Your Hippy friends will love this!

Peace, Love, Color!

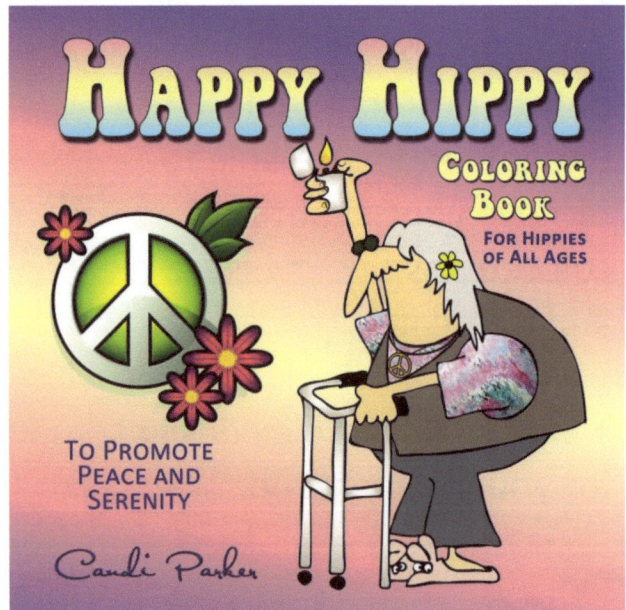

Available now on Amazon.com